In the Name of Allah the Gracious, the Merciful

Moses (عليه السلام)
The Man Who Defeated Armies with His Staff

Copyright © 2022 by Lantern Publications

All rights reserved. No part of this publication may be reproduced, distributed, or transmitted in any form or by any means, including photocopying, recording, or other electronic or mechanical methods, without the prior written permission of the publisher, except in the case of brief quotations embodied in critical reviews and certain other noncommercial uses permitted by copyright law. For permission requests, write to the publisher, addressed "Attention: - Permissions (Moses (عليه السلام) The Man Who Defeated Armies with His Staff)," at the email address below.

A catalogue record for this book is available from the National Library of Australia

Lantern Publications
info@lanternpublications.com
www.lanternkids.com.au

Ordering Information:

Quantity sales. Special discounts are available on quantity purchases by corporations, associations, and others. For details, contact the distributor at the address above.

Written by: Abbass Noureddin | **Illustrated by:** Tahera Amini | **Translated by:** Amal Abdallah | **Edited by:** Dr Abidali Mohamedali

ISBN- 978-1-922583-26-0
Abbreviations used in this book:
(عليه السلام)- Alayhis Salaam – May peace be upon him.

First Edition

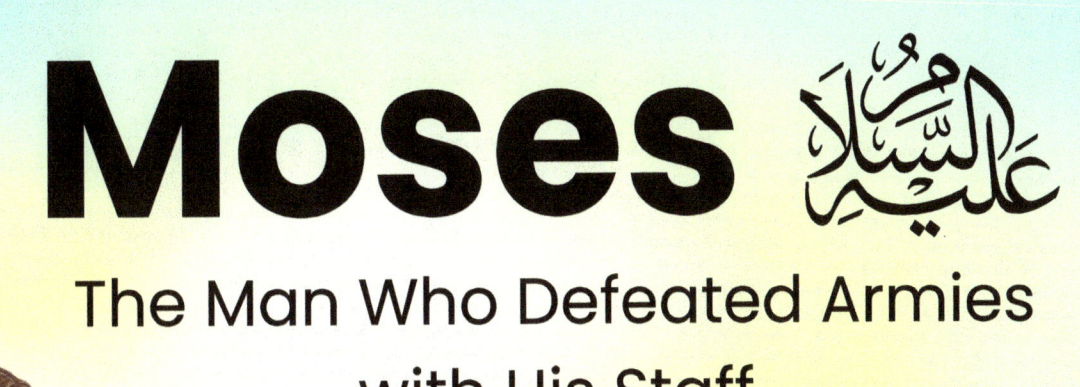

Moses ﷺ

The Man Who Defeated Armies with His Staff

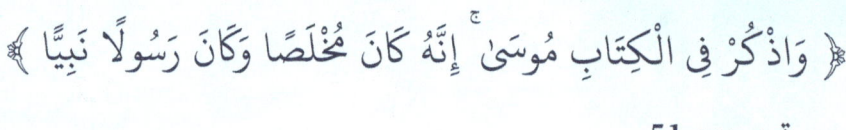

سورة مريم: 51

**"And mention Moses in the Book; surely he was one purified, and he was a messenger, a prophet."
Mary 19:51**

Moses, the son of Imran, was a humble young man. He never saw himself better than any creature.

God wished to demonstrate His great abilities to mankind. He chose Moses, the most humble person for that mission.

However, even after Moses became a prophet, was granted miracles, and accomplished great achievements, he never boasted about anything. Moses always remained humble.

﴿ نَتْلُو عَلَيْكَ مِنْ نَبَإِ مُوسَىٰ وَفِرْعَوْنَ بِالْحَقِّ لِقَوْمٍ يُؤْمِنُونَ ﴾

سورة القصص: 3

"We recite to you from the account of Moses and Pharoh with truth for people who believe."
The Stories 28:3

God, the Almighty, ordered Moses 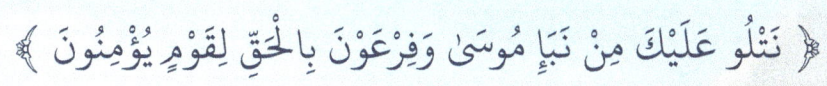 to build a monotheist society, where people worshiped one God only. At that time, the people of Moses were the only monotheist people on the earth, however, they did not live freely. They were enslaved by the pharaohs. They were neither independent nor dignified. They, like most Muslims today, were are controlled by foreigners.

﴿ وَإِذْ قَالَ مُوسَىٰ لِقَوْمِهِ يَا قَوْمِ اذْكُرُوا نِعْمَةَ اللَّهِ عَلَيْكُمْ إِذْ جَعَلَ فِيكُمْ أَنْبِيَاءَ وَجَعَلَكُمْ مُلُوكًا وَآتَاكُمْ مَا لَمْ يُؤْتِ أَحَدًا مِنَ الْعَالَمِينَ ﴾

سورة المائدة: 20

﴿ يَا قَوْمِ ادْخُلُوا الْأَرْضَ الْمُقَدَّسَةَ الَّتِي كَتَبَ اللَّهُ لَكُمْ وَلَا تَرْتَدُّوا عَلَىٰ أَدْبَارِكُمْ فَتَنْقَلِبُوا خَاسِرِينَ ﴾ سورة المائدة: 21

"When Moses said to his people, 'O my people, remember Allah's blessing upon you when He appointed prophets among you, and made you kings, and gave you what none of the nations were given. O my people, enter the Holy Land which Allah has ordained for you, and do not turn your backs, or you will become losers.'" The Table 5:20-21

Moses's ﷺ mission was difficult, because his people were used to slavery and humiliation. Though they led a miserable life, they were not willing to follow him.

Moses told them, "I am God's prophet. He sent me to you. God ordered us to go to the Holy Land and build the state of justice and monotheism."

Their answer was, "If you really are God's prophet, then perform miracles!"

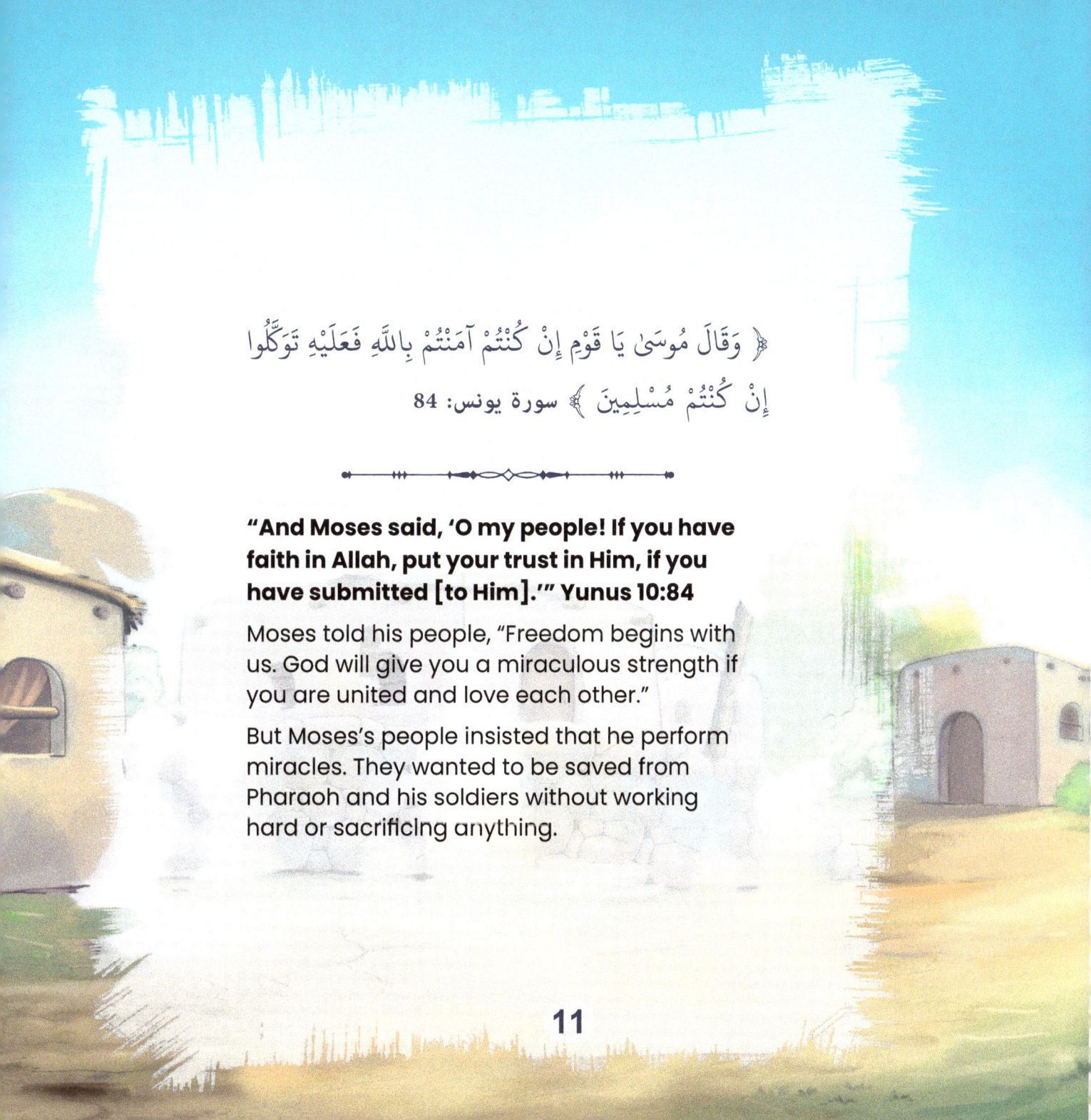

﴿ وَقَالَ مُوسَىٰ يَا قَوْمِ إِنْ كُنْتُمْ آمَنْتُمْ بِاللَّهِ فَعَلَيْهِ تَوَكَّلُوا إِنْ كُنْتُمْ مُسْلِمِينَ ﴾ سورة يونس: 84

"And Moses said, 'O my people! If you have faith in Allah, put your trust in Him, if you have submitted [to Him].'" Yunus 10:84

Moses told his people, "Freedom begins with us. God will give you a miraculous strength if you are united and love each other."

But Moses's people insisted that he perform miracles. They wanted to be saved from Pharaoh and his soldiers without working hard or sacrificing anything.

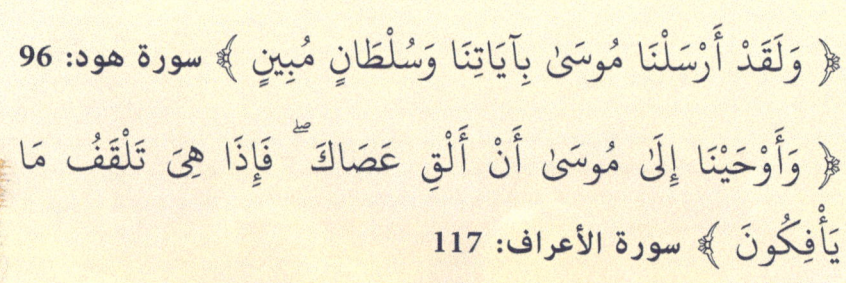

﴿ وَلَقَدْ أَرْسَلْنَا مُوسَىٰ بِآيَاتِنَا وَسُلْطَانٍ مُبِينٍ ﴾ سورة هود: 96

﴿ وَأَوْحَيْنَا إِلَىٰ مُوسَىٰ أَنْ أَلْقِ عَصَاكَ ۖ فَإِذَا هِيَ تَلْقَفُ مَا يَأْفِكُونَ ﴾ سورة الأعراف: 117

"And certainly We sent Musa with Our communications and a clear authority." Hud 11:96

"And We signalled to Moses: 'Throw down your staff.' And behold, it was swallowing what they had faked." The Heights 7:117

Moses ﷺ started demonstrating miracles, and his people saw how he defeated the mighty Pharaoh and humiliated him. Now, the Pharaoh feared a single man, and Moses ﷺ continued to challenge him.

Pharaoh feared for his reign, so he submitted to Moses ﷺ, and agreed to set his people free.

﴿ وَإِذْ فَرَقْنَا بِكُمُ الْبَحْرَ فَأَنْجَيْنَاكُمْ وَأَغْرَقْنَا آلَ فِرْعَوْنَ وَأَنْتُمْ تَنْظُرُونَ ﴾ سورة البقرة: 50

"And when We parted the sea with you, and We delivered you and drowned Pharaoh's clan as you looked on." The Cow 2:50

However, Pharaoh couldn't hold back his anger for long. Soon after he set Moses's people free, rage took over him. He wanted revenge because he saw himself better than Moses ﷺ. He ordered his soldiers to follow Moses's people to the sea, and kill them all!

Moses's ﷺ people thought they were doomed, but then, a miracle happened!

God ordered Moses ﷺ to strike the sea with his staff. The sea was parted, and Moses's ﷺ people safely crossed it!

However, when the foolish Pharaoh followed them with his huge army, God the Almighty, ordered the sea to return to its original state. Pharaoh and all his soldiers drowned.

﴿ قَالَ رَجُلَانِ مِنَ الَّذِينَ يَخَافُونَ أَنْعَمَ اللَّهُ عَلَيْهِمَا ادْخُلُوا عَلَيْهِمُ الْبَابَ فَإِذَا دَخَلْتُمُوهُ فَإِنَّكُمْ غَالِبُونَ وَعَلَى اللَّهِ فَتَوَكَّلُوا إِنْ كُنْتُمْ مُؤْمِنِينَ ﴾ سورة المائدة: 23

﴿ قَالُوا يَا مُوسَىٰ إِنَّا لَنْ نَدْخُلَهَا أَبَدًا مَا دَامُوا فِيهَا ۖ فَاذْهَبْ أَنْتَ وَرَبُّكَ فَقَاتِلَا إِنَّا هَاهُنَا قَاعِدُونَ ﴾ سورة المائدة: 24

"Said two men from among those who were Godfearing and whom Allah had blessed: 'Go at them by the gate! For once, you have entered it, you will be victors. Put your trust in Allah, should you be faithful.' They said, 'O Moses, we will never enter it so long as they remain in it. Go ahead, you and your Lord, and fight! We will be sitting right here.'" The Table 5:23-24

When Moses ﷺ and his people reached the Holy Land, they found a tyrannical people in it. God ordered Moses ﷺ to enter the Holy Land together with his people, in order to build the state of justice. But the people of Moses ﷺ were scared and stepped back.

They told Moses, "Go ahead, you and your Lord, and fight these tyrants! We do not want to fight!"

They were used to Moses ﷺ fighting their battles, and had not learned a lesson from the miracles Moses ﷺ revealed. They needed to know what real strength is.

﴿ قَالَ فَإِنَّهَا مُحَرَّمَةٌ عَلَيْهِمْ أَرْبَعِينَ سَنَةً ۛ يَتِيهُونَ فِي الْأَرْضِ ۚ فَلَا تَأْسَ عَلَى الْقَوْمِ الْفَاسِقِينَ ﴾ سورة المائدة: 26

﴿ وَظَلَّلْنَا عَلَيْكُمُ الْغَمَامَ وَأَنْزَلْنَا عَلَيْكُمُ الْمَنَّ وَالسَّلْوَىٰ ۖ كُلُوا مِنْ طَيِّبَاتِ مَا رَزَقْنَاكُمْ ۖ وَمَا ظَلَمُونَا وَلَٰكِنْ كَانُوا أَنْفُسَهُمْ يَظْلِمُونَ ﴾ سورة البقرة: 57

"He said, 'It shall be forbidden them for forty years: they shall wander about in the earth. So do not grieve for the transgressing lot.'" The Table 5:26

"We shaded you with clouds, and sent down to you manna and quails [saying]: 'Eat of the good things We have provided for you.' And they did not wrong Us, but they used to wrong [only] themselves." The Cow 2:57

Because Moses's people disobeyed him, and insisted on not fighting their enemy, they wandered aimlessly in the desert for fourty years! However, God was kind to them, and wanted to give them another chance.

In that desert, God sent down to them the most delicious food and the best drink and clothes, which they enjoyed without effort.

﴿ قَالَ مُوسَىٰ لِقَوْمِهِ اسْتَعِينُوا بِاللَّهِ وَاصْبِرُوا ۖ إِنَّ الْأَرْضَ لِلَّهِ يُورِثُهَا مَن يَشَاءُ مِنْ عِبَادِهِ ۖ وَالْعَاقِبَةُ لِلْمُتَّقِينَ ﴾

سورة الأعراف: 128

"Moses said to his people, 'Turn to Allah for help and be patient. The earth indeed belongs to Allah, and He gives its inheritance to whomever He wishes of His servants, and the outcome will be in favour of the Godwary.'" The Heights 7:128

Moses used to tell his people, "You should fight your enemy to become dignified. God saved you from slavery and captivity, sheltered you from the burning desert sun, and offered you the best food. You must be thankful to God, and build a state of monotheism and justice, so that people know God's greatness and become monotheists like you."

﴿ سَأَصْرِفُ عَنْ آيَاتِيَ الَّذِينَ يَتَكَبَّرُونَ فِي الْأَرْضِ بِغَيْرِ الْحَقِّ وَإِن يَرَوْا كُلَّ آيَةٍ لَّا يُؤْمِنُوا بِهَا وَإِن يَرَوْا سَبِيلَ الرُّشْدِ لَا يَتَّخِذُوهُ سَبِيلًا وَإِن يَرَوْا سَبِيلَ الْغَيِّ يَتَّخِذُوهُ سَبِيلًا ۚ ذَٰلِكَ بِأَنَّهُمْ كَذَّبُوا بِآيَاتِنَا وَكَانُوا عَنْهَا غَافِلِينَ ﴾

سورة الأعراف: 146

"Soon I shall turn away from My signs those who are unduly arrogant in the earth: [even] though they should see every sign, they will not believe in it, and if they see the way of rectitude they will not take it as [their] way, and if they see the way of error they will take it as [their] way. That is because they deny Our signs and are oblivious to them." The Heights 7:146

However, the people of Moses ﷺ became arrogant and boastful.

They saw themselves better than the rest of the people. They forgot that it was God who favored them and gave them all the miracles. And so, they were no longer fit to receive God's extra mercy and grace.

﴿ رَبِّ إِنِّي لِمَا أَنْزَلْتَ إِلَيَّ مِنْ خَيْرٍ فَقِيرٌ ﴾

سورة القصص: 24

"My Lord! I am indeed in need of any good You may send down to me!"
The Stories 28:24

Moses ﷺ was given great miracles. He defeated Pharaoh and his army by himself. He parted the sea with his staff. Yet, he never saw himself better than anyone, but rather became more humble.

Certainly, only the humble one who loves people and seeks for their guidance, will be given the best abilities.

www.ingramcontent.com/pod-product-compliance
Lightning Source LLC
Chambersburg PA
CBHW051251110526
44588CB00025B/2958